# FOOTBALL
# SAFETY

**DiscoverRoo**
An Imprint of Pop!
popbooksonline.com

Robert Cooper

abdobooks.com

Published by Pop!, a division of ABDO, PO Box 398166, Minneapolis, Minnesota 55439. Copyright © 2020 by POP, LLC. International copyrights reserved in all countries. No part of this book may be reproduced in any form without written permission from the publisher. Pop!™ is a trademark and logo of POP, LLC.

Printed in the United States of America, North Mankato, Minnesota.

052019
092019

THIS BOOK CONTAINS
RECYCLED MATERIALS

Cover Photos: Shutterstock Images, (helmet), (pads); iStockphoto, (shoe and football)

Interior Photos: Shutterstock Images, I (helmet), I (pads), 7, 9, 11, 12, 19, 20, 21, 28, 30; iStockphoto, I (shoe and football), 6, 13, 17, 18, 31; Mike Roemer/AP Images, 5; John Bazemore/AP Images, 8; Adrian Kraus/AP Images, 14–15; AP Images, 22; Pro Football Hall of Fame/AP Images, 23 (top); Vernon Biever/AP Images, 23 (bottom); Stephen B. Morton/AP Images, 25; Scott Boehm /AP Images, 26; Ben Margot/AP Images, 27; G. Newman Lowrance/AP Images, 29

Editor: Nick Rebman
Series Designer: Jake Nordby
Library of Congress Control Number: 2018964842
Publisher's Cataloging-in-Publication Data
Names: Cooper, Robert, author.
Title: Football safety / by Robert Cooper.
Description: Minneapolis, Minnesota : Pop!, 2020 | Series: Football in America | Includes online resources and index.
Identifiers: ISBN 9781532163746 (lib. bdg.) | ISBN 9781644940471 (pbk.) | ISBN 9781532165184 (ebook)
Subjects: LCSH: Football--Juvenile literature. | American football--Juvenile literature. | Safety--Juvenile literature. | Sports--Safety measures--Juvenile literature.
Classification: DDC 796.3320--dc23

# WELCOME TO
# DiscoverRoo!

Pop open this book and you'll find QR codes loaded

with information, so you can learn even more!

Scan this code* and others

like it while you read, or visit

the website below to make

this book pop!

# popbooksonline.com/football-safety

*Scanning QR codes requires a web-enabled smart device with a QR code reader app and a camera.

# TABLE OF CONTENTS

# CHAPTER 1
# MAKING FOOTBALL SAFE

The quarterback is ready to pass the ball. Green Bay Packers defender Clay Matthews races toward him. Then Matthews slams him hard to the ground. It's a **sack**! But there's a flag on the play.

WATCH A VIDEO HERE!

*Clay Matthews prepares to tackle Minnesota Vikings quarterback Kirk Cousins during a 2018 game.*

The referee called a penalty. Matthews

hit the quarterback too hard.

*Most injuries happen when players collide.*

Football players **collide** on every play. Muscle injuries are common. And in recent years, head injuries have become a big concern.

Football leagues are working to make the game safer. New rules limit hard hits. Also, players cannot use their helmets to hit opponents.

**DID YOU KNOW?**

**Players practice tackling by using a large pad. It is called a tackling dummy.**

*Dummies help players practice safe tackling.*

Players practice the best way to
tackle. This helps limit injuries. Teams
also limit the number of full-contact

*Los Angeles Rams
quarterback Jared
Goff takes part in
a practice without
full pads.*

*A player runs with the ball during a flag football game.*

practices. Instead, they practice without pads and do not tackle one another.

## FLAG FOOTBALL

Many doctors believe kids should not play tackle football when they are young. They worry that kids will hurt their heads. Flag football is a popular alternative. There is no tackling in flag football. Instead, players grab flags hanging from opponents' waists. As a result, players have fewer injuries.

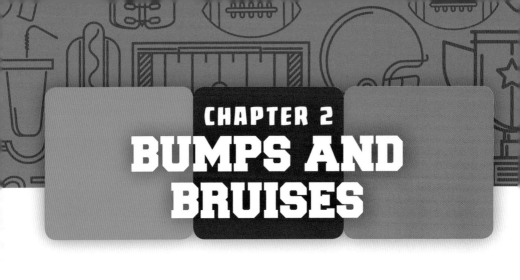

# CHAPTER 2
# BUMPS AND BRUISES

Football is a game with lots of contact.

Defensive linemen **charge**. Offensive

linemen try to block them. The running

back races up the field. A defender slams

him to the ground. Every football play is

**COMPLETE AN ACTIVITY HERE!**

*A defender delivers a powerful hit during a college football game.*

rough. Players can injure just about any

body part.

Some injuries are more common for certain players. For instance, running backs cut back and forth across the field. They may hurt the **ligaments** in their knees. Linemen get more shoulder injuries. These players spend the whole game pushing and shoving.

# MOST COMMON FOOTBALL INJURIES

Head

Shoulder

Knee

Foot/ankle

Clemson Tigers coaches help a player off the field after a concussion.

One of the most common injuries is a concussion. This injury is caused by a hard hit to the head. The hit harms the player's brain. Concussions can be dangerous. In some cases, they can even be deadly. Teams take concussions very seriously.

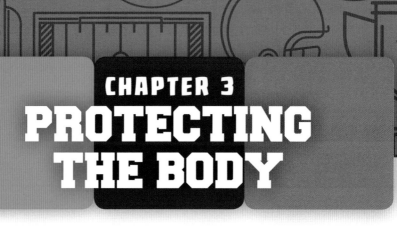

# CHAPTER 3
# PROTECTING THE BODY

Football players wear lots of gear to protect themselves. Safety starts at the top with a helmet. A **face mask** protects the eyes and mouth. To protect their teeth, players wear mouth guards.

LEARN MORE HERE!

*A helmet has pads inside that help soften the blow from hits.*

**DID YOU KNOW?**

**Players wore leather helmets in the early 1900s.**

Players also wear pads on their bodies. They wear shoulder pads, thigh pads, and knee pads. These are the areas where players get hit the most. The pads go under a player's uniform. They help players stay safe during big hits.

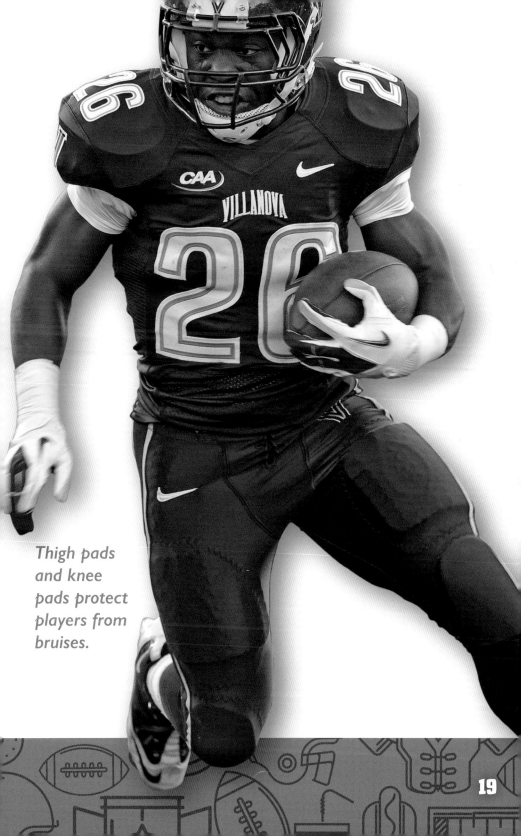

Thigh pads and knee pads protect players from bruises.

*Linemen take hits on almost every play.*

Wide receivers wear smaller pads so they can run faster. Linemen wear thicker pads because of all the hits they take. Some linemen also wear knee

braces to protect themselves even more.

However, even the best pads can't keep a

player totally safe.

*A brace helps support the knee and can reduce the risk of injury.*

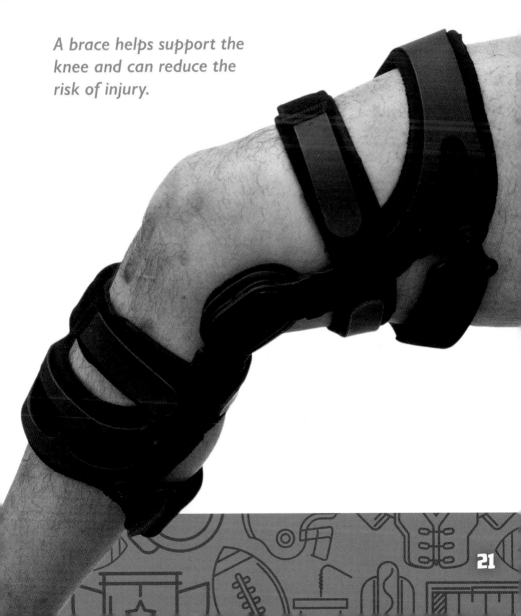

# TIMELINE

**1869**
The first college football game is played. None of the players wear helmets.

**1877**
A college student makes the first shoulder pads.

**1880**
Players begin wearing pants with pads in them to protect their legs.

**1910s**
Leather helmets become common.

**1939**
College players are required to wear helmets during games.

**1950s**
Face masks become common.

CHAPTER 4

# CHAPTER 4
# GETTING HEALTHY

Football players often have minor injuries. **Trainers** help treat those injuries. Doctors might also treat players when injuries are more serious. Some doctors specialize in certain parts of the body, such as the knee. For the worst injuries, players may need surgery.

Jacksonville Jaguars trainers help a player after an injury.

LEARN MORE HERE!

A trainer puts a bandage on a player's arm.

Many small injuries don't require a player to sit out. Trainers put bandages on cuts or bruises. Or they can put braces on sore joints. But more serious injuries can force a player to miss up to a year of football. One example is a tear of the muscles in the knee.

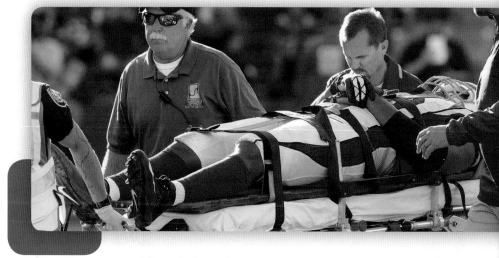

*If an injury is serious, trainers may put the player on a stretcher.*

Players work hard to stay healthy.

That way, they can stay on the field.

Players stretch to avoid muscle injuries.

*Many football players lift weights during the summer to stay in shape.*

*Players sit in an ice bath after practice.*

They lift weights to stay strong. Healthy

eating keeps players in good shape too.

**DID YOU KNOW?**

**Some players sit in ice baths after practice. These baths help their bodies cool down and heal faster.**

# MAKING CONNECTIONS

### TEXT-TO-SELF

Football is a very physical sport. Would you ever want to play football? Why or why not?

### TEXT-TO-TEXT

Have you read about the risks of playing other sports? How do the risks of playing football compare?

### TEXT-TO-WORLD

Millions of people play football each year. Why do you think they play the game even though it can be dangerous?

# GLOSSARY

**charge** – to run at something quickly.

**collide** – to crash together at a high speed.

**face mask** – a piece on the front of a football helmet that protects a player's face.

**ligament** – a tissue that connects the ends of bones.

**sack** – when a defensive player tackles a quarterback who is trying to pass.

**trainer** – a person who helps athletes stay in the best physical shape.

# INDEX

# ONLINE RESOURCES

# popbooksonline.com

Scan this code* and others like it while you read, or visit the website below to make this book pop!

## popbooksonline.com/football-safety

*Scanning QR codes requires a web-enabled smart device with a QR code reader app and a camera.